SNAKES

First published in Canada by Whitecap Books
351 Lynn Avenue, North Vancouver, British Columbia, V7J 2C4

Text and illustration copyright © Random House Australia Pty
Ltd, 2000

ISBN 1-55285-069-2

Children's Publisher: Linsay Knight
Series Editor: Marie-Louise Taylor
Managing Editor: Derek Barton
Art Directors: Carolyn Hewitson and Vicky Short
Design concept: Stan Lamond
Production Manager: Linda Watchorn

Illustrators: Dr David Kirshner, pages 6–19, 26–35, 38–41, 44–55;
Kim Graham, pages 20–25, 36–37, 42–43, 56–57
Consultant: Dr David Kirshner
Academic Consultant: Professor Richard Shine
Writer: Margaret McPhee
Educational Consultant: Tanya Dalgleish

Film separation by Pica Colour Separation Overseas Pte Ltd,
Singapore
Printed in Hong Kong by Sing Cheong Printing Co. Ltd.

For permission to reproduce any of the illustrations in this book,
please contact Children's Publishing at Random House Australia,
20 Alfred Street, Milsons Point. NSW 2061. fax: 612 9955 3381

When you see a word in **bold** type, you'll find its
meaning in the Glossary at the back of the book.

SNAKES

Consultant **Dr David Kirshner**
Illustrators **Dr David Kirshner**
& Kim Graham

WHITECAP
B O O K S

CONTENTS

CONTENTS

World of snakes

Snakes come in many shapes, sizes and colours and are found all around the world.

WHY ARE SNAKES SCARY?

Snakes are feared by just about everybody, yet most people know very little about them. Perhaps we fear snakes because they move without legs. Perhaps it is because some have a **venomous** bite. In this book you will see that snakes are fascinating and should be respected instead of hated.

Head of a reticulated python, the world's longest snake.

The python is life size. How would you feel if it turned its head to look at you?

What is a snake?

*Snakes are **reptiles** like their relatives the lizards, alligators and turtles. Reptiles have scales, lay eggs on land and have a backbone.*

Both the lizards on this page have visible ear openings. Snakes do not.

legless lizard

snake eel

Eels are fish. They have a long fin along the back.

earthworm

LOOK AGAIN!

Though they all look similar, only the blind snake and the sand boa are really snakes.

blind snake

SNAKE LOOK-ALIKES

Unlike most reptiles, snakes do not have legs, but not all long, legless animals are snakes. Earthworms do not have a backbone. Eels are fish, with slimy skin and gills to breathe under water. Caecilians are **amphibians**, like frogs. Some lizards have tiny legs, or no legs, and look like snakes. Worm lizards are not lizards and are not snakes—their scales are different and they do not have a forked tongue.

glass lizard

A snake cannot drop its tail like a lizard.

The worm lizard has scales which go around its body in rings.

worm lizard

The caecilian has wet skin that is ringed like a worm.

caecilian

sand boa

Where do snakes come from?

Snakes and legless lizards have many things in common.
Studying legless lizards helps scientists understand snakes.

BECOMING A SNAKE

Snakes **evolved** from lizards. Many types of lizard have lost their legs through evolution and snakes seem to have started as a type of legless lizard. They evolved from a lizard group similar to the living monitor lizards (pictured centre). Pythons and boas are closest of all to their lizard ancestors. Most legless lizards lost their legs because this makes it easier to burrow underground or to crawl in grass. Snakes may also have lost their legs to crawl underground, but some scientists think it was to help them swim in water more easily. Snakes have a hard, clear scale over their eyes instead of eyelids. They may have developed these 'goggles' when they first burrowed underground or swam in water. Some lizards and their legless relatives are pictured here.

alligator lizard

European glass lizard

Relatives of the alligator lizard lost their legs and became glass lizards.

gecko

flap-footed lizard

girdled lizard

LOOK AGAIN!

Of these lizards, only the monitor lizard has a long forked tongue like a snake.

African grass lizards evolved from girdled lizards.

grass lizard

monitor lizard

Snakes, like the boa constrictor, evolved from lizards similar to the monitor.

a
nstrictor

burrowing skink

ap-footed lizards
ve only small flaps
show they
olved from geckoes.

Burrowing skinks once had fully formed limbs like this water skink.

water skink

11

Necks and tails

Even though snakes appear to be just one long body, they do have necks and tails. Some even have tiny bones where their lizard ancestors had limbs.

BODY PARTS

The snake's neck begins where its head ends. It is usually easy to see this by the angle of the jaws. Where the neck ends is harder to see from the outside, but on the inside, it is where the heart and the main part of the lungs begin. Unlike lizards 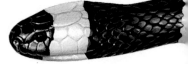 snakes have very short tails starting immediately after the **cloaca** (the opening for waste and mating). On some snakes, such as boas and pythons, the tiny tail is quite noticeable from above at the end of the thick body.

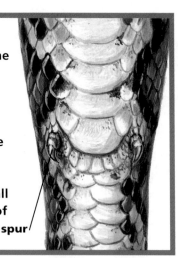

Scales near the tail, on the underside of a Burmese python. The spurs on the sides, and the tiny bones beneath the surface, are all that remain of hind legs. **spur**

neck

body

The tail starts at the cloaca.

cloaca

Broad belly scales change to
pairs of scales on the tail.

Body scales
are small.

An eastern coral snake, from North
America. Most coral snakes are brightly
banded, to warn predators that they
are very venomous, and
should be left alone.

A snake's smooth,
overlapping scales help
it to move easily.

A snake's body is much longer
than its tail. Legless lizards have
a longer tail than body.

Inside a snake

The bones and internal organs of a snake are all designed to fit along its long, thin body.

ALL BACKBONE AND RIBS

The skeleton of a snake is made up of a skull, a long backbone, ribs and a short tail. Snakes have more **vertebrae** (the bones that make up the backbone) than any other animal. This makes them very flexible. A snake has hundreds of ribs. They start at the neck and go all the way to the start of its tail.

The ribs, together with muscles on the underside of the snake make a strong tube to protect its internal organs. In a snake these are long and positioned one after the other, to fit into its long body shape.

Unlike snakes, we have two, almost equal-sized lungs. The liver, which is long in snakes, is more compressed in humans. Humans have a pair of kidneys, each shaped like a bean. The two snake kidneys are shaped like long sausages.

lungs

liver

stomach

position of kidneys (near back)

intestines

hear

left lung

liver

right lu

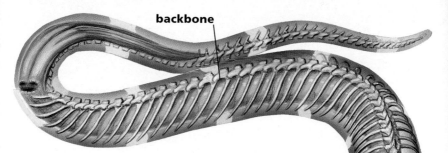

backbone

The backbone and ribs extend along the entire body, but only the backbone reaches the tip of the tail.

kidney

intestines

The intestines of a snake are long and fairly straight. In humans, they are coiled and crammed into a short space.

intestines

The left lung is usually tiny. In some snakes it has completely disappeared, so the right lung does the work of two.

Only some of the skeleton is shown, at the head and at the tail ends. Humans have twelve pairs of ribs. A snake may have more than one hundred pairs.

15

Moving without legs

For an animal to move, it must push against something. Feet push against the ground, fins push against water, wings push against air. Snakes do not have limbs, so instead, they push with their bodies.

Snakes cannot move well on a slippery surface, because there is nothing for them to push against.

The edges of the wide belly scales may help with grip.

A leopard snake crawls along a log by pushing the curves of its body against the rough bark.

GETTING ALONG

Snakes have four main ways of moving. A snake can wriggle along by curving its long flexible body into loops, and then having each loop push against something to send it forward. On a loose surface like sand or mud, a snake can move by anchoring its head and tail, then throwing the middle part of its body forward. It then brings its head and tail into line. This is called sidewinding. Some snakes move by stretching the front part of their body forward, then bringing up the back part. This is called concertina movement. Others creep along in a straight line like a caterpillar, by pushing their belly scales forward into the ground.

The flexible body uses bumps and crevices for leverage.

LOOK AGAIN!

Turn the book sideways. You will see that the snake is actually crawling up a tree.

Snake skin

Although the polished, shiny skin of some snakes makes them look slimy, all snakes have dry and scaly skin.

OFF WITH THE OLD

Every part of a snake's body is covered with scales, including the eyes. Snake scales, unlike the scales of fish, are firmly attached to the skin and cannot be scraped off. Snake scales are made of sections of hardened skin. The outer layer of the skin of snakes, like that of humans, consists of dead cells which must be shed as the snake grows. In snakes, the entire layer of old skin is shed at one time. When the new skin is ready, the snake secretes a fluid under the old skin to make it easier for it to wriggle out. Large snakes sometimes soak themselves in water to make the skin softer and easier to shed.

Fluid under the old skin makes it look dull and bluish.

Cloudy eyes, caused by fluid under the scales, make it difficult for the snake to see. It is often irritable at this time.

The old skin is rolled back inside out like a sock rolled down the leg. It is usually shed in one piece. Sometimes faint traces of the snake's pattern can be seen in the shed skin.

The new skin is shiny and the markings are brighter.

A mandarin ratsnake before, during and after shedding its skin.

When the snake is ready to shed its skin, it rubs its snout on something rough. This snake has managed to catch the skin of its lower lip on a piece of wood and is using the wood to help it crawl out of its skin.

LOOK AGAIN!

The scales covering the snake's eyes are shed with the rest of the skin.

Are snakes really cold-blooded?

Snakes are called **cold-blooded.** *This means they do not make their own heat, like* **mammals** *and birds. Instead, their body temperature is the same as their surroundings.*

SUMMER

All animals must keep their bodies at the right temperature to digest food and allow them to keep moving. Snakes are most active in summer, when they can warm up in the sun. In summer, the so-called 'cold-blooded' snake is rarely cold at all!

WINTER

In cold climates with a long winter, snakes, and other small animals unable to make their own body heat, must wait in the shelter of underground burrows until the warm weather returns. The body temperature of snakes can drop to just above freezing. They remain inactive for months, and because they are not moving, do not need to eat, but instead live off stored fat. This does not harm the snakes at all.

LOOK AGAIN!

Only the squirrel makes its own body heat, so only the squirrel is active in winter.

fox snake

American toad

The large eyes and horizontal pupils of the long-nosed tree snake give it extremely good sight for grabbing prey.

LOOK AGAIN!

To help it swim faster, the sea snake's body is flat and its tail is shaped like a paddle.

This tree snake rarely, if ever, comes down to the ground. With its long, lightweight body it can slide along thin branches and stretch from one branch to another. Its bright green colour blends in with the leaves.

The horned viper is coloured like the desert it lives in.

The horned viper is able to move across loose sand by sidewinding, and only a small part of its body touches the hot surface. The snake often buries itself, leaving only its eyes showing, to lie in wait for prey. Its 'horns' stop the eyes being covered in sand.

Where do snakes live?

Snakes live in almost every part of the world and in almost every type of climate. Some live in jungle trees, some live in deserts, some live in water.

FITTING IN

About the only place snakes do not live is in the frozen lands near the North and South Poles and many islands. Over millions of years snakes have gradually changed their body shape to suit the many different places they live. Some have become long and slender for crawling along thin branches. Some are broad and short for moving across sand. Snakes that live in water have a very long lung and can stay underwater for up to two hours. The nostrils are closed tight to keep out water.

The sea snake has special glands to rid its body of excess salt.

The sea snake's bright colours are a warning that it is highly venomous. This protects it from predators, who have learnt to leave it alone.

The yellow-bellied sea snake drifts across the ocean with the currents. It lives on fish which seek shelter under floating objects, including the snake. When the fish are near its head, the snake makes a sudden sideways snap with its long jaws.

Double takes

*Snakes in similar environments in different parts of the world can look almost identical even though they are not closely related. This is because they have made similar changes to fit into similar surroundings. This is called **convergent evolution**.*

SAME PROBLEM, SAME SOLUTION

The horned viper of Africa and the sidewinder rattlesnake of North America both live in hot sandy deserts. Both have made the same sort of changes to suit the place they live. Both have 'horns' which may keep sand off the eyes when the snake is buried. Both move by sidewinding. And both are a mottled sandy colour.

The identical coiled position of both snakes allows them to collect dew and rainwater in their folds for drinking.

green tree python

MATCHING PAIRS

The green tree python of New Guinea and the emerald tree boa of South America live on opposite sides of the world, yet they are so similar, it is difficult to tell them apart. Both snakes live high in the trees of tropical rainforests and feed mainly on birds. Both are slender and muscular. Both are green with yellow lips and light markings along the back. Both have long teeth for holding their prey through a layer of feathers.

Although green tree pythons lay eggs, and baby boas are born as tiny snakes, the young of both are brightly coloured and different to their parents. Baby boas are red, yellow or green. Baby pythons are red, yellow or brown.

LOOK AGAIN!
The boa has a longer face and a more regular pattern of markings on its back.

emerald tree boa

The bright colours of the young may be to scare off predators. Bright colours usually mean danger.

On a rainforest floor in tropical Asia, three snakes track down their prey.

The king cobra mainly eats other snakes.

Snakes can smell with their tongues.

It is unusual for snakes to eat only other snakes.

The banded krait also feeds mainly on snakes.

What do snakes eat?

Snakes are hunters. Their food is other animals, large and small, which they kill. This is called their prey.

FLESH-EATERS

All snakes are **carnivorous**, which means they only eat meat. Animals mostly eaten are mammals such as rats, rabbits, squirrels and bats, other reptiles, birds, fish, and all kinds of eggs. Some large snakes eat creatures as big as a leopard, smaller snakes eat animals such as snails and even tiny termites. Snakes kill their own food and don't eat anything killed by other animals. Some snakes eat a variety of animals, but others eat only one kind. Some snakes only eat the eggs of other creatures. Because their jaws are built for swallowing, not for chewing or tearing, snakes usually eat their prey whole and usually head-first.

The striped keelback usually eats frogs, such as this painted frog. It also eats fish.

LOOK AGAIN!

Prey is usually swallowed whole. These snakes would easily fit inside one another.

Hunting for food

Snakes hunt alone. Some search for prey then chase it down. Some wait for prey to come to them. Some wait, then chase.

THE QUICK AND THE LAZY

The body of a snake is often shaped for the hunting it does. Active hunters usually have a long, thin body to move after their prey quickly. Ambush hunters have heavier bodies and are well **camouflaged**. Some even lure prey with their tail.

The large eyes and thin shape of this taipan are typical of active daytime hunters.

The gaboon viper of Africa may wait a long time to ambush its prey.

LOOK
AGAIN!

Camouflaged in the leaf litter, a young Mexican cantil is using its tail as a lure.

Finding food

For most snakes, smell and sight are the most important senses for finding food and avoiding enemies. They can also pick up vibrations from the ground, but have no ears.

SNAKE SENSES

A snake does not smell with nostrils, but instead 'tastes' the air or ground, with its forked tongue by picking up tiny particles. It then puts these particles into a special part on the roof of its mouth called **Jacobson's organ** which tells the snake exactly what it is smelling. Some snakes have heat-sensing pits below their eyes or on their lips for finding warm-blooded prey in the dark.

The rattlesnake's heat sensing pits let it 'see' warm-blooded prey, such as the rat, in the dark. The gecko, a reptile and so cold-blooded, is not easily detected.

WHAT SNAKES AND HUMANS SEE

LIGHTS OFF, WHAT HUMANS SEE

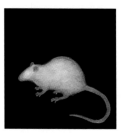

LIGHTS OFF, WHAT THE RATTLESNAKE SEES

eastern
diamondback
rattlesnake,
a pit viper

Large eyes with
cat-like vertical
pupils help the
rattlesnake see
when it isn't
completely dark.

Heat-sensing pits send
messages to the same
part of the snake's brain
as the eyes do. The snake
probably 'sees' a thermal
(heat) image of its prey.

The nostrils are used
for breathing and play
no role in smelling.

LOOK
AGAIN!

Although the snake
can't see the gecko, it
can smell it with
its tongue.

A snake must know
where its prey is
before it can attack.

The forked tongue
is collecting
information.

In for the kill

Once a snake has found its prey, the next task is to kill it. A snake can do this in one of three ways. It can squeeze it to death, it can inject poison or it can simply eat its prey alive.

SQUEEZE AND SQUEEZE AGAIN

Many snakes use **constriction** (squeezing) to kill. They wrap themselves around their prey, squeezing tighter each time the stricken animal breathes out, so that it quickly suffocates or its blood flow is stopped. Instead of wrapping and squeezing, some snakes just push their prey into the ground with one of their coils. Other snakes inject **venom** (poison) into the muscle of their prey with their **fangs** (long, sharp teeth). They then leave the prey to die of the venom or hold onto it until it dies.

An eastern diamondback rattlesnake with jaws almost at full stretch to strike at a brown rat. The long sharp fangs will stab through the rat's fur so the snake can inject its venom.

Venomous snakes have fangs.

When the snak bites, poison i pushed throug its hollow fang

THIS PAGE CAN BE REMOVED

INVESTIGATE

A California king snake squeezing the life out of a southern alligator lizard. Constrictors usually bite down on their prey before they wrap around it, to hold the prey in place. Constricting snakes are usually not venomous, so they often do not have fangs.

An eastern hognose snake swallowing a Fowler's toad.

LOOK AGAIN!

Each snake is using its mouth. Even the king snake is holding the lizard in its mouth.

The toad has inflated its body with air to make it difficult to swallow. The snake will puncture it with special fangs.

How do snakes swallow prey?

Snakes are not able to rip their prey apart, or chew it into pieces, so must swallow it whole. As the prey is often very large, the snake needs special teeth and jaws.

OPEN WIDE

A snake may wait a long time for a meal so when it does find food, it is best if it eats as much as possible. This means it often has to swallow prey that is bigger than its head. To do this the snake has a flexible skull with loosely jointed jaws that open wider than the jaws of just about any other animal. As well, the snake's lower jaw is in two parts. It can stretch sideways, and each side of the jaw can be moved on its own. The snake swallows prey by sinking the teeth of one side of the jaw into the prey. It then pulls that jaw back and extends the other side forward to repeat the process. Slowly, but surely, the prey is pulled down the snake's throat.

The teeth of most snakes are long, thin and sharp. They point backwards into the mouth to make sure prey goes in that direction only. Teeth often break off in the prey. It is very important for the snake to have a good set of teeth, so lost teeth are quickly replaced. New teeth are continually growing next to existing teeth. Therefore, most snakes have only half their possible number of teeth at any one time.

PYTHON SKULL

When not in use the teeth are covered by strong, protective gums.

A Burmese python with mouth shut and open. The jaws can stetch even wider apart than shown here.

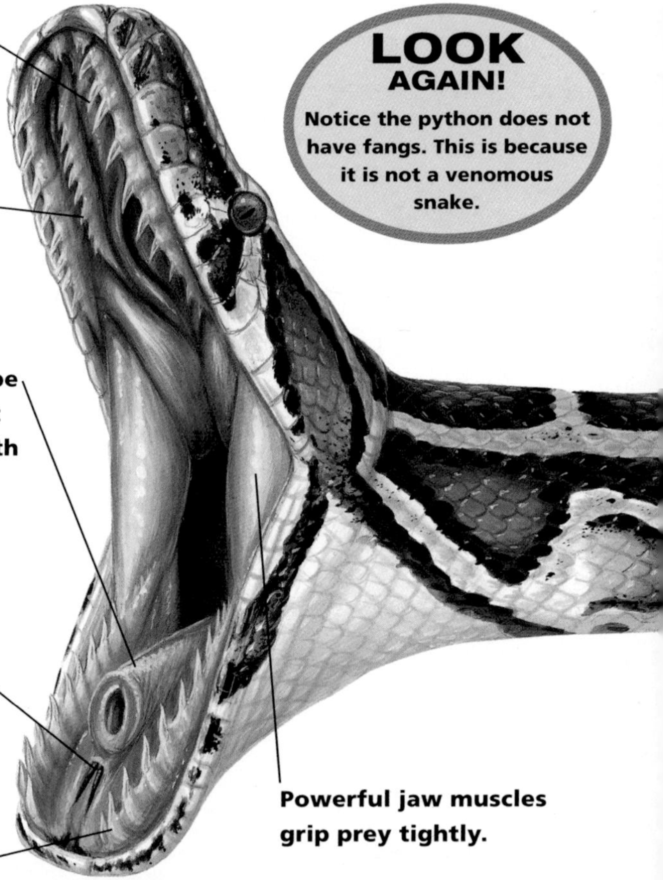

Sharp teeth curve backwards.

Extra rows of teeth help to grip prey.

The windpipe can be moved to the front or side of the mouth to act as a snorkel so the snake can breathe while swallowing.

The sensitive tongue can be withdrawn.

protective gums

LOOK AGAIN!
Notice the python does not have fangs. This is because it is not a venomous snake.

Powerful jaw muscles grip prey tightly.

35

How much do snakes eat?

The amount snakes eat depends on their size and the climate. Some eat small, regular meals. Others eat big meals but less often.

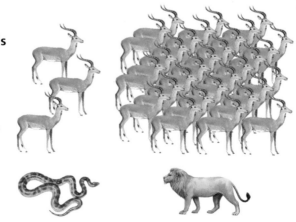

A lion (a warm-blooded **predator**) needs to eat about 30 impalas a year (5 kilograms of meat a day) to stay alive while an African python could survive eating only three or fewer.

FOOD FOR THOUGHT

Snakes do not need as much food as animals like mammals and birds that need it to make energy to heat up their own bodies. Snakes use the sun to warm up their bodies. Snakes are more active and eat more when the temperature is warm. They stay inactive for long periods when it is cold, not using up energy, and so not needing much food. A snake living in a tropical climate will eat more than one living in a cool climate. During winter, in all but the hottest tropics, snakes eat little or no food at all.

African rock python

The largest snake meal ever recorded was a 59 kilogram (130 pounds) impala eaten by a 5 metre (16 feet) African rock python. This is rare, for even these snakes usually eat much smaller prey.

short-toed
(serpent)
eagle

Strong claw
can hold the
snake to the
ground, while t
sharp beak tea
at the snake.

What eats snakes?

In the wild, most animals are at risk of being eaten by other animals. Snakes are no exception.

A DANGEROUS WORLD

Most carnivores will eat a snake if they get a chance. A mongoose will kill and eat snakes, so will cats, foxes, raccoons and even wild pigs. Large frogs have been known to swallow small snakes, as have crocodiles, alligators and large lizards. Other snakes can also be a snake's greatest enemy. Snakes with a 'king' in their name such as king snake, king brown and king cobra, tend to be snake eaters. But the most dangerous predators for snakes are birds, such as eagles. They circle above, swooping down when they spot a snake on the ground to grab it with sharp claws or talons. Powerful wings allow an eagle to carry off even heavy prey and the bird's sharp curved beak can cut through the scaly skin of the snake.

The short-toed or serpent eagle feeds mostly on reptiles, particularly snakes, and will even attack a venomous species like this Indian cobra.

Indian cobra

LOOK
AGAIN!

The cobra spreads its hood in an attempt to scare off the eagle with its large eye spots.

Self-defence

Snakes can defend themselves in a number of ways. Most hide or flee first, but if they cannot escape, they try to scare off their attacker.

AVOIDING ENEMIES

Hiding camouflaged is the best defence. Snakes without the benefit of camouflage will flee. If this fails, some snakes can change their body shape to make themselves look fearsome to frighten off the attacker. Cobras and some other snakes spread their hood to look larger, other snakes rear up in an 'S' shape. Some snakes hiss or use other sounds. Bright colours warn predators that the snake is venomous. Some snakes bluff by looking or acting like a more dangerous snake. Biting is the last resort.

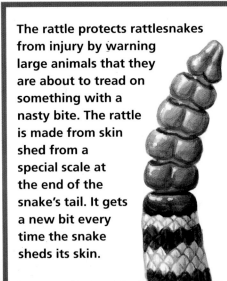

The rattle protects rattlesnakes from injury by warning large animals that they are about to tread on something with a nasty bite. The rattle is made from skin shed from a special scale at the end of the snake's tail. It gets a new bit every time the snake sheds its skin.

2. When cornered, most snakes try hissing, and looking large and scary. This rinkhals has spread its neck into a hood.

1. Snakes usually avoid trouble by hiding or crawling away.

A rinkhals, a venomous snake from southern Africa, shows some of the ways snakes defend themselves.

3. For the rinkhals the next step is to spit venom into the attacker's eyes.

4. When all else fails, most snakes bite.

6. The snake stays 'dead' until the attacker leaves, then goes back to its first defence mechanism—fleeing.

5. The rhinkals and some other snakes flip on their back and pretend to be dead.

Are snakes endangered?

Like many other wild animals, snakes are in danger from humans destroying the places they live, and from hunters who kill them for food, for their skins or out of hatred.

THREATS TO SNAKES

Humans kill huge numbers of snakes. Sometimes this is deliberate. Some snakes are killed because people fear them. Many more are killed for their beautifully patterned skins. Hunters can kill thousands of snakes in a few days. People pay high prices for boots, bags, belts and other goods made of fine snake skin. In some countries snakes are killed for food or to make medicine from parts of their bodies. What kills most snakes, however, is losing the land they live on. Spreading cities, towns and farms are a great threat to snakes because they destroy the places snakes live. Even something as simple as people taking rocks from the countryside to use in their gardens can make life more difficult for snakes, because they use rocks for shelter. Some snakes are now so rare they might die out altogether.

In some countries snakes are killed for traditional medicines.

In rich countries demand for luxury goods like handbags and boots is increasing so that some snake species are in danger of extinction.

Clearing forests to build roads or towns causes many snakes to lose their homes. The San Francisco garter snake has a small habitat area and has 'become endangered' as the city has grown.

San Francisco garter snake

The Malagasy giant hognose, like the distantly related hognose snakes of North America, has an upturned snout to dig up toads.

Malagasy giant hognose snakes

BIG MALES, LITTLE FEMALES

The males of some snake species grow larger than the females. These males fight each other for the right to mate with available females. Larger males are better able to win these fights. Snake fights are like wrestling matches, with the males wrapping around each other and trying to push each other's head down. In some species the males rear up as they try to push each other down, sometimes rising so high that it looks as if they are dancing. In other species the males wrap around each other so tightly that it looks more like a knotted rope. Fighting snakes may hiss but rarely bite. The loser of a contest will simply leave. The winner gets the female.

Fighting and mating

Female snakes advertise for mates by spreading scents.
Sometimes males fight for these females.

BIG FEMALES, LITTLE MALES

Male and female snakes usually look like each other except that females often grow larger to produce more and healthier eggs or babies. Male snakes can find females by their scent from a long distance away. Mating begins when the male wraps his tail, and sometimes part of his body, around the female so their cloacas are side by side.

These Malagasy giant hognose snakes are fighting, not mating!

How do snakes reproduce?

Most snakes lay eggs from which the baby snakes hatch. Some produce live baby snakes in a sac. Either way, the young usually emerge into the world three to five months after their parents mate.

LEATHERY EGGS

Eggs must be kept at the right temperature to **incubate** successfully. Some snakes lay eggs where they can catch the sun's warmth. Some lay eggs in rotting logs or other vegetation which makes heat as it decays. Unlike a hen egg, which has a hard shell, snake egg shells are leathery. Some baby snakes have an **egg tooth** on their nose to cut open the tough shell. This egg tooth disappears soon after the **hatchling** emerges.

After the parents have mated, the young of egg-laying snakes, like this diamond python, may spend three or so months in their mother's body, then another two or so months in the egg before hatching.

The young of live-bearing snakes, like this puff adder, spend a long time, up to five months or more, inside the mother but leave the egg sac as soon as they are out of the mother's body.

LIVELY BIRTHS

Snakes that carry their young inside their body can bask in the sun to make sure the babies get the warmth they need to develop. This is important for snakes in cold areas where eggs would only get a small amount of warmth from the sun each day. The mother snake can also protect the young inside while she moves around, which is easier than having to stay near a nest of eggs. A disadvantage is that the extra weight of the young inside her body makes it more difficult for the mother to hunt for food, as well as increasing the risk of her being caught by a predator.

Raising young

Snakes, like most reptiles, do not usually look after their young. Once a baby snake wriggles out of its egg or birth sac, it is able to care for itself.

MOTHER CARE

Most egg-laying snake mothers leave once they have chosen a nest and laid the eggs. But some stay with the eggs. Mother cobras stay near their eggs and protect them for most or all of the incubation period. Mother pythons not only wrap themselves around the eggs, but also keep the eggs warm by using a special 'shivering' movement that raises the temperature. This is a rare ability for a supposedly 'cold-blooded' animal. Live-bearing snakes look after their young by keeping the young inside the mother. Once the mother gives birth, the baby snakes break out of their sacs and must look after themselves.

Discoloured eggs usually do not produce a hatchling. The mother avoids wrapping round them to prevent the decaying egg spreading fungus to the good eggs.

A female blood python **brooding** her clutch of eggs.

LOOK AGAIN!

Look closely and you'll see that one of the hatchlings has slit its egg with its egg tooth.

Weird and wonderful

Although snakes are all basically the same shape—long, legless and cylindrical—there is a remarkable range of sizes, colours and patterns. And some snakes are very odd-looking indeed.

The slow-moving tentacled snake of Asia attaches itself to underwater plants and feeds on fish. The tentacles help with camouflage by breaking up the outline of the snake's head.

female

EXTRAORDINARY SNOUTS

Snakes living in different places have evolved different features to help them fit in and find food. The most curious variations of all are in the shape and decoration of the head—the feeding end—and are to help with catching food, camouflage and burrowing. Three of the more bizarre examples are shown here.

male

The leaf-nosed snake of Madagascar (an island near the coast of Africa) gets its name from the long growth on its nose. This, and the snake's twig-like colour, make it very hard to see. The nose of the female is more elaborate and leaf-like than that of the male.

The flattened nose of the quill-snouted snake is used to burrow through sand in search of its favourite food, worm lizards.

Record breakers

Who are the record holders of the snake world?

SNAKE EXTREMES

The longest snake in the world is the reticulated python at up to 10 metres (33 feet). The heaviest is the green anaconda which is almost as long as the reticulated python and can weigh up to 250 kilograms (550 pounds). By contrast, some members of the thread snake family are so tiny they are no thicker than a pencil lead. Snakes that live longest are the pythons and boas. In captivity they can live for more than forty years. The gaboon viper of tropical Africa holds the record for the longest fangs at 5 centimetres (2 inches). All of these snakes can be seen in this book (look in the index).

The most venomous land snake is the small-scaled snake, or inland taipan, of central Australia. The venom carried by a single snake is strong enough to kill a quarter of a million mice.

Black mambas are not black but have a black mouth.

actual size

The saw-scaled snake is the most dangerous snake in the world. Unlike sea snakes and the small-scaled snake, which has stronger venom, it is short tempered and is found in densely populated areas.

black-headed sea snake

actual size

fastest land
ake is the black
amba. It can reach
top speed of
0 kilometres
12 miles) an hour.

Some scientists claim that sea snakes are the most venomous of all. But they are rarely aggressive.

Found in Africa, the Middle East and India, this snake's bite causes thousands of deaths each year.

Kinds of snakes

Australian blind snake

*There are around 2700 species of snakes. They are sorted into groups called **families**. Scientists don't agree on which snakes belong in each family.*

MAIN SNAKE GROUPS

Worm and blind snakes: These three families of small, primitive, cylindrical, burrowing snakes are found in warmer parts around the world. **Boas and pythons:** These snakes live in warm areas, are small to very large, mostly heavy-bodied and kill prey by constriction. **File snakes:** These snakes have loose skin and rough scales for holding fish prey. They are found in Asia and northern Australia. **Shieldtails and pipe snakes:** These two families of primitive burrowing snakes with short blunt tails are found in tropical Asia and South America. **Sunbeam snake:** This family has only one species which lives in Southeast Asia. It has very shiny scales and burrows into the earth. **Colubrids or typical snakes:** This is the largest family of snakes and is found in most parts of the world. It has a huge variety of shapes and sizes. Most are harmless, but some are venomous. **Elapids (cobras and their relatives):** These venomous land and sea snakes are found in warmer parts of the world. **Vipers and pit vipers:** These are short, heavy-bodied snakes with long fangs which fold back to fit into the mouth.

checkered garter snake (a colubrid)

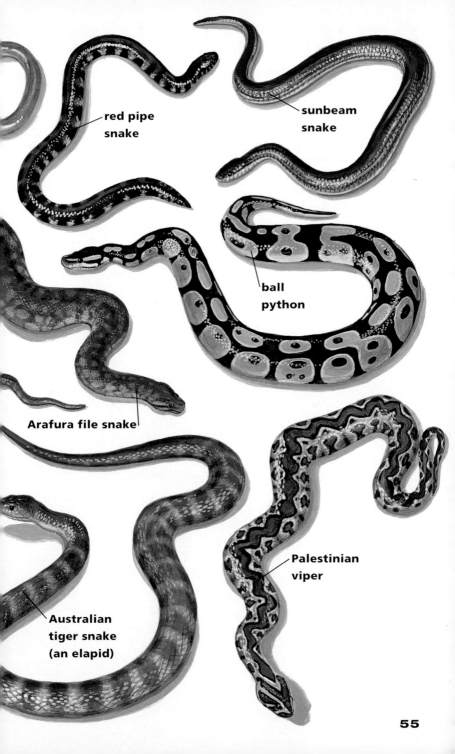

red pipe snake

sunbeam snake

ball python

Arafura file snake

Australian tiger snake (an elapid)

Palestinian viper

An anaconda in your bathtub?

Some snakes can be kept as pets, others are best left alone.
An anaconda is one snake that is best left alone!

NOT MUCH FUN

What would it be like to keep a full-size anconda in your bathtub?
For a start, the bathtub might not be big enough. Green anacondas
grow up to 10 metres (33 feet) and weigh up to 250 kilograms
(550 pounds). They live in the tropics so
you'll have to keep your bathroom
hot, around 30°C (85°F). You'll have
trouble finding food. An
anaconda can eat an adult
caiman (a type of alligator) or
a pig every two to three weeks.
And they're not even
particularly friendly, especially
when they're hungry—you'd
need to keep the family dog
well away!

Make your own snake mobile

1. Choose a snake from this book and draw a picture of it coiled up with its head in the middle of the drawing.

2. Choose a skin pattern from this book. Draw the pattern on both sides of the paper and colour it in.

3. Colour in the snake's eyes and scales—and fangs if you want to show them.

4. Now cut out the snake's outline and attach a piece of string to the head. Hang it up so that it slowly spirals.

GLOSSARY

amphibian An animal with a backbone that develops in the water but spends most of its adult life on land, such as a frog.

brooding Sitting on eggs so they stay at the right temperature for hatching.

camouflage (KAM-a-flahzh) The colours, patterns or body shape that helps an animal blend in with its surroundings.

carnivore (kar-niv-or) Eats meat.

cloaca (clo-AK-ah) The opening through which waste products are passed and which is also used for reproduction.

cold-blooded Having a body temperature that is the same as the surroundings.

colubrids The biggest snake group. Colubrids are mostly harmless.

constriction The way some snakes kill. A constrictor coils its body around its prey to squeeze and suffocate it or cause bloodflow to stop.

constrictor A snake that coils its body tightly around its prey to kill it.

convergent evolution The development of similar features and habits in animals which are not related, because they live in similar environments, find similar food and face similar problems.

egg tooth A small sharp tooth which hatchling snakes use to slit open the egg.

elapids A group of poisonous snakes. It includes cobras and mambas.

environment The features of the place where an animal or a plant lives that influence the way it lives.

evolve To change gradually through generations. Animals and plants usually evolve to better adapt themselves for the environmental conditions in which they live.

fang A long, pointed hollow or grooved tooth which may be used to deliver venom to prey.

hatchling A young animal newly emerged from an egg.

incubate (IN-kew-bate) Keeping an egg at the right temperature for the time

GLOSSARY

between when it is laid and when it hatches (the incubation period).

Jacobson's organ Pits on the roof of a snake's mouth into which the tongue places scent particles.

mammals Warm-blooded animals that are usually covered with hair and whose young feed on milk from the mother's teat.

membrane Soft, thin skin.

pits Heat sensors below the eyes or on the lips of a snake for finding warm-blooded prey in the dark.

predator An animal that hunts and kills other animals for food.

prey An animal that is hunted and killed as food by another animal.

rainforest A forest which is usually wet and steamy all through the year.

reptiles Animals that do not produce their own body heat, usually lays eggs on land, have scales and have a backbone.

skeleton The bones of the body that supports the soft tissue.

venom Poisonous liquid used to kill prey. It is delivered by the fangs.

venomous Able to inflict a poisonous sting or bite.

vertebrae (VER-ta-bray) An odd-shaped bone with a circular centre, many of which join together to form the neck, backbone and tail of an animal.

warm-blooded An animal that makes its own body heat, such as a bird or a mammal.

FIND OUT MORE ABOUT SNAKES

BOOKS

Behler, John L, and King, Wawyne, *The Audubon Society Field Guide to North American Reptiles and Amphibians,* Alfred A. Knopf.

Brazaitis, Peter, and Watanabe, Myrna, *Snakes of the World,* Mallard, New York,1992.

Carmichael, Pete, and Williams, Winston, *Florida's Fabulous Reptiles and Amphibians,* World Publications, Tampa, 1991.

Cogger, Hal, *Reptiles and Amphibians of Australia,* Reed, Sydney, 1992.

Marais, Johan, *Snakes,* Grange Books, London, 1997.

Mattison, Chris, *Snake,* Dorling Kindersley, London, 1999.

Mattison, Chris, *The Encyclopedia of Snakes,* Blandford, London, 1995.

Spellerburg, Ian, and McKerchar, Marit, *Mysteries and Marvels of the Reptile World,* Usborne Publishing, London, 1984.

Taylor, Barbara, *Snakes,* Lorenz Books, London, 1998.

Wiedensaul, Scott, *Snakes of the World,* Quintet, London, 1991.

WEBSITES

http://www.arazpa.org.au/links.htm

http://vhsociety.home.mindspring.com/links.htm

http://www.herper.com/sneha/herpetology.html

http://www.links2go.com

http://www.lizardlover.com

http://home.ptd.net/~herplink/index.html

CLUBS

Society for the Study of Amphibians and Reptiles, United States. http://www.ukans.edu/~ssar/

INDEX

INDEX

NDEX

POSTER!

Collect all 6 of the gold  stickers

(you will find one on the stickers' page in each book)

**Send all 6 stickers on a sheet of paper
along with your name and address to:**

Investigate Series Poster
Whitecap Books
351 Lynn Avenue
North Vancouver
British Columbia
V7J 2C4

and we'll send you your free  **series poster.**

Please allow 21 days for delivery.

COMING SOON

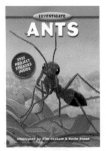
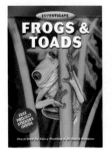